Ways of Love

A Poetry Collection

by

William Waldorf

Ways of Love – A Poetry Collection
poems © William Waldorf
Published by Prolific Pulse Press LLC
ProlificPulse.com

Library of Congress Control Number: 2023922418

ISBN   Paperback 978-1-962374-06-4
ISBN   EBook 978-1-962374-07-1

Published November 2023
Raleigh North Carolina USA

Photo Credit: Unsplash

TABLE OF CONTENTS

DEDICATION VI

A Grandfather's Gift vi

ACKNOWLEDGEMENTS VII

Draw of Love 1

A Lover A Hero.. 2

One was Blushing... 3

Non-Est Perfectum Hominem 4

Why Surrender 5

Beauty I 6

Beauty II 7

The Gift of a Pearl 8

Distance 9

An Angel 10

Legs and Rain.. 11

Bananas/Lovers.. 12

A Bedtime Poem 13

Mistress and Maid.. 14

Wild Iris... 15

A Wandering or Longing 16

Again... 17

One.. 18

A Rose 19

Flight of Feathers 20

A Pillow... 21

Let Us Turn our Lights Down Low 22

Still 23

Passion I 24

Passion II 25

Passion's Melody 26

Pure Love 27

For Eternity 28

One More Day 29

Love's Bounty 30

Love's Misery 31

Affection's Loss 32

Heart Sighs a Breath 33

Zeus' Marriage Gift 34

Party Notes 35

Loves Humor 36

Love Fragrances on Valentine's Day 37

Blind Comfortable Love 39

Cautious Love 40

To Find Love 41

Reply 42

There They Were Lips 43

Gloom Day 44

Emotion or Passion 45

Two Hands 46

Musical Bliss 47

Welcome Surrender 48

The Search 49

Paradox 50

My Love Can't Write a Poem for Me 51

ABOUT THE AUTHOR 52

DEDICATION

To my grandchildren Matthew and Jules

A Grandfather's Gift

I cradle you tightly and gently prance
with lyrics in my head from past critics
to remind what's a required response to
your generation

Love requires safety for eternity
don't want lack of basic needs to panic
you. Fear may appear when your sips briefly
delay. I'll teach patience with love's support

Give relief as gas escapes from my tap
you'll know my scent while we dance to music
pray you hear my hum sung soft at meal time
to help you learn how to drift into sleep

A life with music offers you beauty.
Time opens your eyes to color and shape.
Even now we share laughter together
while I pray for more years to watch you grow

When I go as I must I hope and trust
I've taught you how to recall me someday
to keep love alive here to stay with you
while my spirit watches you sleep and dream

ACKNOWLEDGEMENTS

Thank you to the following publications for including my poetry:

"A Pillow," "Draw of Love," "One," *The Thursday Poets' Anthology, Dreams & Realities.* 2022

"Draw of Love" published by *Ravens Quoth Press, Editor's Choice Collection PSYTHUR 1*, October 2023

In the writing of this book, I have been sustained by the kindness of many people.

My writing groups:

US1 Poets, Sunday Morning Poet Group consisting of: Ginny Pina, Joan Menapace, Nancy Demme, Rod Richards, Robert Berry, and Anne Christensen. A special thanks to Creative Fiction workshops, whose Elliot M. Rubin, Humanist & Poet's friendship I value.

All sounding boards for my work.

Most important is my wife Jane who constantly is asked to listen at most inconvenient times. Of course, Zoom for the ability to develop international relationships with other poets such as Sarfraz Ahmed who resides in London, England.

Draw of Love

There are moments lovers of all ages
relish the attention, yet feel caution
deep within their hearts since being smitten
with hope. What will be their future chances?

Unable to be apart— absences
pull like magnets with enormous tension.
Not to be included or feel certain
will make most flinch as partners need glances.

They'll look in another's eyes to be sure
that their love's relationship will endure
no matter what obstacles encountered.
Together they'll never feel outnumbered.

With time the power of love grows stronger
as lovers find comfort with each other.

A Lover A Hero

A view more beautiful than the twinkle
of the light in the night from fireflies' glow,
as they search for lovers to find a beau,
is the moonlight that highlights an angel.

Everywhere in the air, such loud babble
I need a lover I need a hero
all scramble to satisfy libido
But uncontrolled passion can be frightful.

Unless this abandon is welcome, shared
by consenting adults no longer scared.
Then join your passion in love's greatest bliss
be attentive—pray, you'll never remiss,

to spend eternity locked in happiness
as you enjoy your sweet angel's kisses.

One was Blushing

Early in the morn as I spied
two small brown birds jumped before me
one was blushing red like a bride.

Head twisted looking starry-eyed
while the smaller moved adroitly
early in the morn as I spied

Nature's courtship being applied
gatherings piled, like a dowry,
one was blushing red like a bride.

Eyeing the pile of seeds supplied
singing loudly with so much glee
early in the morn as I spied.

Two speckled red finches outside
a gift of nature just for me,
one was blushing red like a bride.

Watching them perching side by side
made me feel so very happy.
Early in the morn as I spied
one was blushing red like a bride.

Non-Est Perfectum Hominem
(There is no perfect man)

I struggle with perfect like an addict.
I fumble and grapple with every trial
not perfectly done. Then I would grumble
to myself panicked often feeling licked.

I'm cursed with obsessive behavior.
In retrospect when I go to review
forced along my compulsive avenue
I'll hunger for a different future.

A mother's love is pure, free from blemish
but all others I've learned to admonish.
Be wary, I've spent my life in this search,
not one on earth showed up in my research.

All imperfect humans should learn practice
makes progress; then they'll become less anxious.

Why Surrender

love should not be a test you encounter
but a guide to understand both your hearts
approach gently each with utmost support
equal works better than a surrender

if interlocked toes lose warmth together
their reaction seems like forced emotion
lean, thin like a crushed pillow's condition
deflated unprepared to surrender

your bruised heart groans like an evicted guest
who stands alone as ice winds chill their chest
you remember with a jolt: not my fault
those good past times were lost from your assault

careful if love feels like a surrender
you might have caught only a pretender

Beauty I

Beauty's gestures are quick like butterflies
that will sit upon the frailest flower
gentle, lighter than the smallest feather
whose thin stem does not break like a disguise.

Hair that heaven highlights with natural light
as it bounces with the slightest movement,
to return, without need for adjustment,
when my heart flutters with so much delight,

'til I stand hand in hand next to love's side
then, like balm is applied I'm satisfied.
Eagerly my heart knows love has begun.
I pray it never will become undone.

No longer curious why calm captured me
I'll join bliss with my beloved eternally.

Beauty II

She moves
like a butterfly
gentle
small
as a feather
on a frail flower
its stem bends with life's weight
does not break
in this
ballet
as my arm slips around her arched waist
in an embrace
of
love

The Gift of a Pearl

When it is worn a pearl grows more luster
as it gathers love being on display,
its iridescent blush may seem risqué
while it graces the neck of its wearer,

with elegance to make all its capture.
For it seeks love not as a quick buffet
but life together as the main entrée
whether single or placed in a cluster,

never underestimate their power.
Strong more beautiful than any flower,
be sure to appreciate the value
this gift will imbue.

Or forever search for that true lover,
their gift of pearls, will help you discover.

Distance

Youth plucked as if stolen from family
from safety, in the army volunteered
into service war, I'm broken hearted
feel alone but prays that God hears my plea,

If I will serve faithfully and proudly
please protect my love from getting weakened
with time as I fear being rejected
by distance with a post, summarily.

For absence can increase my love's desire
but distance may make it weak to acquire
Only my words are what's available
I'll send kisses inside each syllable

for you to daily bridge deep distances
and to encourage back rapid responses

An Angel

A view more beautiful than the twinkle
of the light in the night from fireflies' glow,
as they search lovers to find them a beau,
is the moonlight that highlights their angel.

Everywhere in the air, such loud babble
I need a lover I need a hero
all scramble to satisfy libido
But uncontrolled passion can be frightful.

Unless this abandon will be returned, shared
as lovers enjoy both pleasures declared
with passion to relish their greatest bliss
be attentive—pray, you're never remiss,

to spend eternity locked in happiness
as you enjoy your sweet angel's kisses.

Legs and Rain

On my walk greeted by drizzle,
steam rises.

Soft wet drops remind me
of kisses, when
long muscle-toned legs pass me.

Her hair flows, soaked skin, glistens
with sweat, my eyes take my brain away
to my youth.

Those legs disappear into my future.
I struggle to possess their image
despite tears.

I wish for the Sun's return
in the rain.

Bananas/Lovers

A bunch of bananas lay on the counter
curled together green, firm to the touch.

As they sit their peel softens and yellows,
almost gold. Their gift turns from a chewy
hard meal to surrender into softer
flesh.

When left to age sugar marks will show
time lost as peel browns like lost collagen.

It turns soft, black and the inside firm meat
becomes mush, syrupy, soon discarded
after they attract several small fruit flies

that flit like elusive memories do
until in time they will be forgotten.

A Bedtime Poem

Let's share a little rhyme or two O.K.?
It could be a sonnet or just one stanza
when I write its always my agenda
since I enjoy the meter and wordplay,

beats of rhythm with rhyme are my entrée
to a story or song filled with drama,
old love, grief, or view of a begonia
are to me, like presents on my birthday.

When you read this gift of mine just reflect
take some time after all it's just a rhyme
gifts to enjoy or discard just select
but I hope you'll remember me sometime.

For poems are meant to
be shared beyond two.

Mistress and Maid
After the painting by Painter Johannes Vermeer

Vermeer's eye tugs at our imagination
when we meet women of varied station,
shown by their dresses of contrast, color,
and design, as both appear to wonder,

about a white note right in the center.
Since they're focused there— a love letter
perhaps? A lighted leopard trimmed mistress
in yellow dress, seems hesitant, cautious,

deep in thought with her hand upon her chin,
as her maid waits about to speak, turned in
front of inkwells shown from her black backspace,
as is the painter's custom with his space.

Comfortable with those placed in poses
you should join others to sing his praises.

Wild Iris

Sufferance with perseverance through portal's
of death. Lessons may scrub fundamentals
as you shudder when it's wisp will linger
to recall terror, you might remember.

When you become conscious of some noises
that seem to float out there on precious air.
To rest and press the earth's dark dry surface
as it cools tremors, expand no longer
tenacious, pugnacious, or contentious,
as life
free
rushes
to relish the pale sun.

Where on an azure sea of light,
it floats
through mist
pulsates.

Will its allure
regenerate
from oblivion
life's essence

A Wandering or Longing

One morn as I stood on the desert sands
of Albuquerque and saw strange snow swirls
as if Van Gogh stroked the sky suddenly
with white ridges like whorls dust the land
inside this framed freckled hot horizon
where three mounds protruded
from the sand like pearls.

Guarded by a Saguaro's bright beauty
stood up from its green top as if just cued
there, was a bright sunlit cactus flower
whose bold yellow petals relished the sun,
while pleats expanded from snows trickle pools.

Together we shared this day as if one
blizzards, flowers so rare under that sun.
like children who received love sparingly
will act like a Saguaro slow to reach their maturity.

Again

A heart
surprised
by a familiar
look
can   pause
breath
when lovers recall
that
wellspring
of what
complete
feels like
a newborn's weight
upon
a mothers
bosom
then   perhaps
they'll lose
a need
for access
to egress
and
welcome
love
again

One

Alone on my own is my fate.
I have none to collaborate
with or hear laughter shared.
Seems strange to miss this emotion.
Sounds are gone as if they're stolen,
a fact for the unpaired

who live within past memories,
like when we ate some blueberries
whose sweet-tart taste lingered,
calling us for most of the day.
Now your spirit sings everyday
to a lonely songbird

who aches for disappeared music
to join, to hear his lost critic.
This all changed since you're gone.
There are no echoes in my life.
Quiet is like a dull kitchen knife
that won't cut clean when drawn.

A Rose

A bright red rose, inside your wrist
newly drawn, placed beneath the skin
deep, sharp, vibrant, and permanent
act of rebellion or statement?

Either choice will give you trouble,
it can't be undone now clearly.
Is it puffed up from the needle
should be answered immediately?

Was that a nervous laugh I heard
as you stare in disbelief,
at blood oozing from a green leaf,
everything seems so absurd.

On your wrist for all to notice
you used your skin as a canvas,
some wonder if you lost focus
others may think it is madness.

Your action was impetuous,
etched and branded like those cattle.
sometimes in life you can stumble,
to be caught by love's forgiveness.

Flight of Feathers

Sufferance has become my acquaintance
since your heart denied my love's admittance
the moment you found more from another
made me wonder about a past gesture

you shared with me when you breathlessly blared
our love could never ever be compared,
then you rolled over me in ecstasy
to embrace me oh so passionately.

How did your love's ardor evaporate
so quickly to not have to hesitate
when you choose partners faster than rumors
spread of free treasures.

Careful my cleaver, fickle, thespian
don't acquire a soiled reputation.

A Pillow…

on my bed

beckons

as I lie down

it will collapse

to support me

   but I rise surprised

   to see it no

swished flat

  love

  must be fluffed

nurtured each day

  as

  you puff

  my heart

Let Us Turn our Lights Down Low

My arm gently cradles your waist
 when I draw you closer
          my heart and breath are no longer
    steady,
                as beauty conquers any thoughts
misplaced.
   Together more than fifty-seven years
            old   tunes   familiar,   words
memorable
        passion feels like before— remarkable.
    We cling
                savor
                    lest it disappears.
                              to become one
              we hold each other
     tonight:
              to steady,
              soothe,
                      a frightened heart
     I will protect
                   from any monster
as before,
        your knight in lover's armor.

Still

Silence can be loud, wouldn't you agree
places its most strong, like a waiting room
there you'll stare at the door too long, maybe

you'll feel as if you've been put in a tomb
where the quiet carries the faintest sound
to your ear as if you're in a belfry

a strange phenomenon may now occur
you'll hear your heart so loud it'll astound
after a while it seems so regular

you could miss a beat or two of cadence
then you'll get that jolt it might seem eerie
when you realize you've heard silence

love's loss frequently gnaws at your stomach
here in the quiet of your bed— you ache.

Passion 1

To crave, to want, to desire, is to need intimacy which
rests on lust's border. But to feel passion
you can avoid love
since ardent passion is not
affection.
Passion
or love
is often interchanged.
Who tries to fill
appetite's vacuum
first, with unconditional touch
then deeds to match
the place and tempo just received.
Ways lovers
communicate their pleasure:
touch me there
                    that's the spot
reciprocate in a minute.

Passion II

When you feel a warm release
then you squeeze
to feel more movement.
Your nails dig, hold,
restrict, the chance passion
would leave.
You struggle to keep feeling this.
This palpitating
ride of love's pleasure—
you refuse,
to let it slip, slide, away.
Savor
down to the last warm trickle,
flushed, drained, winded,
now your grip can relax
passion's meal,
is satiated.

Passion's Melody

You lie on my chest I feel satisfied
embraced by your love is to feel content
infused with power that seems magnified ,
felt but not seen, my hope is your intent

to touch play our violin's concerto
on my body to release melodies,
such crescendos without tranquilities
will undulate with vibrato's tempo.

I abandon restraint for lust's passions
in exchange for sexual explosions.
A pause in duration brings exhaustion
as we collapse from all this exertion.

Our staccato satisfied libido
rests within our private decrescendo.

Pure Love

To lie alongside love is to desire
immortality. Fragrances in air
from fresh brushed tossed hair
will titillate inner passion's bonfire

to warm and ignite, a skin's arousal
from normal emotion as this affair
can intensify when love's hearts ensnare
but fail to slow down being physical.

So amorous you can be ravenous
and recall past feeling from fabulous
Nirvana, your state of pure happiness,
which can remove that hunger's emptiness.

Once you have experienced love's beauty
keep it for a day past eternity.

For Eternity

Love makes your insides burst wanting to share
    such beauty, skin softer than rose petals
    her deep flashing fiery dark eyes wrinkles
with a smile so bright, how should I compare.

sunrise, sunsets seem dull, I will declare
    if one took all the worlds brightest candles
    they wouldn't equal light from those sparkles
greater than heavens' brightest moonlight stare.

I love her deeply her total being
    calms me with happiness, yet in candor
    when I'm away, my body is aching
for the nearness of her, my sweet lover.

If providence ends my life abruptly
my love will remain for eternity.

One More Day

One day we feel the warmth from each other.
Together we surrender to romance
to spend our lives forever as lovers.

One day more we'll feel anticipation,
until we lovers return to embrace
since hours now seem like eternity.

One day more, we're no longer beginners
blended to perfection from affection
through children to a new generation.

One day more as we move a lot slower
through the day our touch continues to say:
Your love fills me with exhilaration

One last day no more we'll share, but prepare,
love's rest for those who time forged as a pair.

Love's Bounty

At first love can be as simple as trust,
like hands wrapped around a warm cup you sip,
slow afraid to burn as sweet brushes lip
to feel heat's distance as thirst adjusts moist.

This first love may be a shared tearful laugh,
Your nervous heart's giggle grows to chortle
from casual to a common model.

A couple's cornerstone to their kickoff
will have tears, laughter, shared in all their years
like a squished pillow requires a new puff
of fresh air from lovers' gentle squeezes
their respect for each should never be tough.

Excitement, spontaneity, give way
but humor keeps love for eternity.

Love's Misery

Gently brush your cheek with my love-struck eyes
as we stroll along to share the sun's warmth,
my hope tucked inside your secure coat's cloth.
You're unaware my misery makes sighs.

You do not see you have my attention.
With each breath you speak my eyes watch your lips,
my heart aches from unspoken intention.
Misery, my dues for this membership.

Oh, so lonely it can be next to you
whose views reflect through me, without value.
Invisible I cry inside my heart,
secretly unable to be apart.

When chains from a love are unrequited,
being alive feels cold and short-sighted.

Affection's Loss

A lonely heart feels cold as an iced pane,
crystal clear no more when love disappears.
Hope fades when vulnerable whisperers
will feed a jealous flame to share such pain.

Those backstabbers who spin faces around
to hide their glee, offer false sympathy
secretly smile at this difficulty.
Others wonder can love ever be found?

Your heart scans past memory solutions:
please find answers to stop loves divisions,
as insecurity chills all 'till numb,
without a warmth connection to welcome.

Lost love is like grief from those forgotten,
who daily mourn hearts' loss of affection.

Heart Sighs a Breath

A lump presses inside against my throat
unable to touch your love anymore.
My mind spins as breath stutters body sore,
lungs struggle for air from a tight garrote,

numb senses bring along their lost control
first with tingles at the base of my spine,
which will steal night's desire to unwind
but be lost in depression's deep hellhole,

to hear loud echoes inside a scared mind.
Death forces grief, trust broken like a thief
but rejection lingers without relief
to feel violated as if I'm blind,

unable to rebound from this dark depth
of existence as my heart sighs a breath.

Zeus' Marriage Gift

Hera, you're my passion for all seasons.
I'll make a circle where you'll be secure
adorned with gifts worthy of your figure.

A swatch of bright red satisfies Lilith,
shuts off her brand of thievery at birth
covered in diamonds to radiate the sun's
power to blind evil eyes, watch them burn.

I'll gather pure ash from a volcano,
add Hade's strength to resist any blow.
Sirens shall imbue a hypnotic sound,
to make all your enemies run aground.

A proud symbol of royal mastery
despite my constant promiscuity,
this ring will bind you for eternity.

Party Notes

A Cheshire's grin means terror to a mouse.
If you will question stranger or strangler
as a dance space shrinks, and you sense danger
tell yourself *I should leave this party house.*

If you feel like the roast duck at dinner
when all want to have her and no other,
then don't be the potato mashed to mush
flat on the plate who waits for fate's last crush.

Take this tutorial: hit phones redial
blurt out loud to your phone I'M COMING HOME
RIGHT NOW, THERE'S NO NEED TO TRACK MY
MOBILE ON MY WAY I'LL BE HOME IN A SHORT
WHILE.

Then make like a tree and leave right away
if you feel uneasy two are better
take a girlfriend don't be an entrée.

Loves Humor

A first love can be as simple as trust,
like hands wrapped around a warm cup you sip,
slow afraid to burn as sweet brushes lip
to feel heat's distance as thirst adjusts thrust.

This first love may be a shared tearful laugh
your nervous heart's giggle grows to chortle
from a casual to unique model.
Here a couple's cornerstone starts their path

where tears, laughter, will be shared in all years
like a squished pillow receives a new puff
of fresh air from lovers' gentle squeezes
then respect for each should never be tough.

Excitement, spontaneity, give way
but humor keeps love for eternity.

Love Fragrances on Valentine's Day

We lived many years
        in love together
                our time often shared
                      if you remember
with gifts of flowers
        Persephone's left
                those brought to Hades
                        when under the earth
haunted fragrances
        wisps linger barely
                beyond reach, torment
                      poor souls with
what's there
      as eyes fill with tears
            then they will taste salt
                a bitter recall
                    lost oceans salt spray
they'll wish to restore
        beyond their black veil
                as they grope blindly
                  and long for loves touch
For Love, only love
        will be remembered
                true lasts forever
                  placed inside your heart
held by crimson bow
        a holy color
                that powers the gods
                  I must speak quickly
to whom I tasted
        relished in their walk,

warmed from their wide smile,
hungered for their scent,
I fear I might not
have more time to speak
afraid I dare not
stop to
lose   more time
I watched as a boy
lovers place their gifts
of flowers inside

books to press petals
flat were they would retain
their natural
sweetness

Blind Comfortable Love

Beauty never fades when viewed by love's eyes
tis the magic of true love's legacy
applied to memory, from ecstasy
while passion pauses to release warm sighs

then they'll catch their breath to begin again.
Since time hides as love's ardor advances,
when exhausted bodies share embraces
subtle changes go unseen by their brain.[1]

Love can miss years to see what was before
for the heart tells the mind what to ignore.
Wrinkles can disappear, hair holds color,
some steps seem harder while they grow older.

Time together can seem like love's award,
but to feel comfort is the best reward.

---

[1] Change blindness is a phenomenon of visual perception that occurs when a
stimulus undergoes a change without being noticed by observer.
.

Cautious Love

To lie alongside love is to desire

      immortality. Fragrances in air

        like fresh washed brushed hair,

          can titillate inner passion's bonfire,

  as skins warm in intimate arousal

       when emotions normal for an affair

        intensify if both act debonair,

      and fail to slow down being physical

               to enter Eden's
    garden   ravenous,

        may soon know the meaning of
dangerous,

       if they ignore responsibility

    they'll learn the world might treat them both
harshly.

Like the aged

     whose attractions might have waned

     often judge others since they feel ordained.

To Find Love

Is he the one who loves me, can it be
as we stand alongside each hand in hand?
We do what tasks each need without command,
to prove our love is not a fantasy.

A magic spell he holds over my will.
When he is angry, God sees I take blows
hide my bruises keep my vow no one knows.
When I am in his arms, I feel the thrill.

My body shudders as he takes pleasure,
from mine, his treasure who shows devotion
when we lie together interwoven
as his muscles draw out loves last measure.

Like a hungry moth is drawn to bright lights
a lonely heart settles rather than fights.

Reply

it's just two words you utter in response

to those three that you always want to hear

from a loved one who shares your elixir

softly spoken without much hesitance

would be a gentle touch, three syllables,

often don't require an acknowledgement

if given will mean more than a review,

two words as when you simply say: me too.

There They Were Lips

                           below eyes that beckoned
when she starred childlike her tongue tip circled
along an open pouted puffed lower lip
where it curled to begin a slow withdrawal
then quickly flick again to tantalize
as her eyelids fell over her sleeplike

she seemed aloof as if in a dream state
vulnerable I couldn't resist slipped
my arm around her waist
pulled her close smelled
her hair against my chest

couldn't take my eyes away
as her mouth rose to meet mine.
I felt her hips press against mine,
her hands on my back as her nails
dung into my flesh to block out the
world as she pulled me tighter
she is a passionate kisser

Brrang Brrang *Oh no don't Wake up go back* damn
it's time for school oh but I will revisit that novel
again
to research for my first real kiss High schools
can have so much tension.

Gloom Day

grey day, splash day solitude begs
as rain clouds tap my umbrella's cover
too many memories from a lover
whose scent of betrayal smells like rotten eggs

inhabits our walls to prevent rebirth
of my ability to love again
as I walk abandoned on wet terrain
to wonder where's, trust for me on this earth

can I find a hug to stop an arm ache
hollow echo repeats beats from heartache
I lose humor as warmth flees like a draft
cold numb like a dementor's dark witchcraft

love is like the taste of chocolate truffles
as they explode taste buds into shambles

Emotion or Passion

Passion or love is often interchanged
but to feel passion can you avoid love
since ardent passion is affection too.
To crave, to want, to desire, is to need
intimacy which rests on lust's border.

Which tries to fill that appetite's vacuum
first with unconditional touch then deeds
to match the place and tempo just received
as lovers communicate their pleasure,
desire for mutual orgasm.

You'll freeze, stop as you feel a warm release
then you'll squeeze, to end any more movement.
Your nails: dig, hold, restrict, the chance passion
would leave, you struggle to keep feeling this.

This palpitating ride of loves pleasure
 which you refuse to let slip, slide, away,
savor it down to the last warm trickle,
winded, flushed drained, now your grip can relax
as passions meal seems to be satiated.

Two Hands

they rest entwined wrinkled
lie still until it's their turn to speak
patient ready with experience
they'll calm all when they speak,

their pat or touch releases love
transform time makes all young
back to their first familiar sound:
Do re mi, you will see
I love you, know I will
always love you

these furrows begin to understand
In these love shares patience
In each shares love

To hold
   memories and perception
      for time begins as hands clasp
        in a furrow's fold

take my hand love,
   remember how we began—
      souls, hearts as two hands
        hold love through time

Musical Bliss

You lie on my chest I feel satisfied
embraced by your love is to feel content
infused with power that seems magnified ,
felt but not seen my hope is your intent,

to touch play our violin's concerto
on my body to release melodies,
such crescendos without tranquilities
will undulate with vibrato's tempo.

I abandon restraint for lust's passions
in exchange for sexual explosions.
A pause in duration brings exhaustion
as we collapse from all this exertion.

Our staccato satisfied libido
rests within our private decrescendo.

Welcome Surrender

You sink into my arms against my chest,
feel you collapse into my warm body,
take my strength offered freely and calmly
for this brief moment is always the best.

When lovers feel support from each other
smell from her washed hair, feel of his rough beard,
these familiar senses should be savored
as past emotions of primal wonder.

You acknowledge loves surrender is true.
A quick interview conveys from a touch,
much as you were able to make each blush.
Responses reflect unforeseen value

when love feels soft, as a cashmere sweater,
never did you expect so much pleasure.

The Search

My body reaches for your touch.
like a leaf turns towards the light
the back of your hand lightly caresses.
along my long soft smooth thighs,
if they'll separate to surrender
to your tactile love's touch
          who
talks to my heart,
       answers   my question:
are your actions true,
or an old, used stall,
with little value
for a future
often a lover,
can   feel   unfulfilled,
     used,
cold.
                  I
search to find a
giver who can hear
my heart's melody
to accompany
as we become
a golden
example of how
love is always
taken care of.

Paradox

More than half a century together
can be years of ecstasy and torture
to love is to experience feeling
content or aching

A hug will reveal if you feel anger.
Is it tight because of something that's said,
or a heart's gift from your loving partner?
If the former, do you wish they were dead?

Ah, that's love's paradox relationship,
hate, love, can exist in the same heart blip.
Time may mellow a reactive response,
that can seem like an air of nonchalance

But that pendulum can start with a crumb
of irritant or swing to love's spasm.

My Love Can't Write a Poem for Me

When I talk about kisses as light
as snow, melt gently upon her soft
warm face, she only feel's cold. To say
her voice is as beautiful as morning's
call from a choir of birds, she
complain about their loud chatter.
if I'll ask, can you feel the meter.
She'll reply can you read it slower.
What about rhyme," oh was it that kind,"
she'll utter? But it doesn't matter to me
as she stacks our clean laundry daily.
Incognizant to stanzas or form, its
more important towels fit
and the ovens shine not rhyme.
Her gift is our dust free house
which she fills tirelessly with
her unselfish love.

ABOUT THE AUTHOR

William "Bill" Waldorf began his love affair with poetry with strict forms like sonnets. Currently he is focused on poems from daily life. He loves to show history has not changed us.

His book, *My Sonnets and More* explores various themes of love relationships with less politics. He focuses on relationships between gender, generations, and lovers. *The Thursday Poets' Anthology-Dreams & Realities,* included several of his poems edited with the regular Thursday poetry critique group.

Reviews are always appreciated. Thank You!

William Waldorf's Amazon Author Central Code